S. Bond

Church Membership

Or the Conditions of New Testament and Methodist Church Membership

Examined and Compared

S. Bond

Church Membership
Or the Conditions of New Testament and Methodist Church Membership Examined and Compared

ISBN/EAN: 9783337260569

Printed in Europe, USA, Canada, Australia, Japan

Cover: Foto ©Lupo / pixelio.de

More available books at **www.hansebooks.com**

CHURCH MEMBERSHIP;

OR,

THE CONDITIONS OF NEW TESTAMENT AND METHODIST CHURCH MEMBERSHIP EXAMINED AND COMPARED.

.

BY S. BOND,

Methodist Minister of the Montreal Conference.

TORONTO :

WILLIAM BRIGGS,

78 & 80 King Street East

MONTREAL: C. W. COATES.   HALIFAX: S. F. HUESTIS.

1882.

PREFACE.

It is a common and natural desire when a man appears before the public in the printed page, to explain the reasons. The Author of this essay has written and published, because of the pressure of a conviction that the subject of it needs to be studied by the people of the Church to which he belongs. He has marked with regret a disposition to ignore the importance of Christian fellowship to the individual Christian; and he has heard many statements as to the relation which it bears to the proper conditions of Church membership, which he believes were made through misconception of what the New Testament teaches on this subject. The views thus expressed tend very directly to make those who hold them feel that the conditions of membership in the Methodist Church are purely arbitrary; and in their application necessarily exclude some who have a right to membership, according to their ideas.

Believing that a correct knowledge of what is the evidence afforded by the New Testament, would remove such feelings, and lead these persons, and many others, to highly prize what now they shun, I have here sought to present a candid statement of its testimony on this interesting, but neglected subject. This object is the writer's excuse for presuming thus publicly to discuss the subject of the following pages. Whether the ability of the treatment, as well as the importance of the subject, justifies his temerity, is for others to determine, if they wish. If conviction of the correctness of the teaching of this essay is produced, and a more general and cheerful use of Christian fellowship follows, I shall be abundantly rewarded.

S. BOND.

INTRODUCTION.

The effects of Christianity on our race is a subject of surpassing interest. The attention need not be confined to those things that are purely spiritual, in order to discover much that is both remarkable and pleasing. In its working and progress among men it has developed many different phases; extending all the way, from the most perfect exhibition of its real nature, down to the most defective, until all that is Christian fades away in worldliness. The same is true in regard to the acceptance of its doctrines. There have been examples of the most cordial and complete belief of what it teaches, and there have been cases of the loosest acceptance of the least portion of divine truth, until it has been indistinguishable. Yet through a large portion of these phases of its working, and indeed perhaps through all, this fact holds true; that each succeeding period has been characterized by a larger measure of grace and truth in the admixture. The worldly character has been more conformed to the Christian, even when the Christian character has been more conformed to the worldly; and the false doctrine has had less of antagonism to the truth as it is in Jesus, or the Christian doctrine has covered a wider range of the human thinking; and error has been confined to a narrower range.

The same relative phases have been produced in the

organic life of the Church. There have been and still are, instances of the most exact and pronounced ecclesiasticism, denying all grace beyond its pale; and there have also been, and still exist instances where divine grace is believed neither to require nor produce any form of ecclesiastical organization. Often these two extremes have come into conflict; while betimes they have been found working side by side, without greatly disturbing each other. They have come even closer than this, and their workings, though silently proceeding, have tended to some form of upheaval.

It is when they work within the same ecclesiastical organization that the conflict becomes dangerous. For the one tends to enforce high-churchism, and the other almost no-churchism. The most important phases of some Church organizations of to-day centre round this point. Methodism has had a quiet struggle for some years within her fold between these two phases of Church doctrine, and Church life. This conflict of opinion in regard to what properly constitutes membership in the Church is not one of external ecclesiastical order, but is doctrinal in its nature. A clear perception of what is the nature of New Testament Church membership will settle in most minds within her enclosure, and in many without, the question of duty in regard to the manner of holding membership in the Church.

In order to aid, if I may, by a candid enquiry into the question as it is presented in the New Testament, I now ask an impartial consideration of the following investigation into the question.

CONTENTS.

CHURCH MEMBERSHIP.

CHAPTER I.

NEW TESTAMENT CHURCH MEMBERSHIP.

What is New Testament Church Membership?

CHRIST taught His disciples, "My kingdom is not of this world;" "The kingdom of God is within you." And yet the Church of the living God is spoken of by Him and His apostles as something that men could see and recognize. He instructs us that the offending brother that will not be reconciled to him who is offended, by private conference or friendly communication with two or three, is to be reported unto "the Church." Paul teaches the spiritual nature of the kingdom of God, saying, "The kingdom of God is not meat and drink, but righteousness, and peace, and joy in the Holy Ghost;" and yet in his history the record is, he went up from Cæsarea to Jerusalem and saluted the Church. To many minds these statements may appear contradictory and inconsistent; and to others they will, perhaps, be confusing. Only to him who comprehends, to some considerable degree, the nature of Christ's work will there be perfect clearness.

But when a man sees that the "new creature" is the thing that is essential, then the mode of divine procedure will explain the order Christ has adopted. By His Spirit he works in man to the production of a

new life, that so influences its subjects as to produce a
brotherhood. This feeling of brotherliness creates a
community, whose members voluntarily submit one to
another, because Christ has wrought in them that
which distinguishes them from all others. They can
at once see that this work of Christ, and this community of brethren, formed by mutual feelings, are
two distinct things. The one has relation to God, and
the other has relation to men. But the former is
always the cause of the latter. Identification with
the community can never give the new life and the
consequent community of feeling. All the organization is the result of the power of Christ upon the heart
and life. To suppose the opposite order of working,
i.e., the formation of the organization for the purpose
of producing the new life, is to suppose what Christ
did not establish. And yet the community, developed
by the new life, was to be an instrument to influence
others to the obtaining of this same new creation.
But its office was always to be merely instrumental ;
the new creation was always a divine work.

Here then, we have the idea in its most concrete
form—the Church is a community of saved persons,
drawn together by divine life in them, and governed
by Christ's law as revealed in the New Testament. In
the progress of the divine work, where the life is the
essential thing, and the organization is but the casket
to hold the precious treasure, there is almost of
necessity some divergence of these two separate
things. We see them separated in fact, and we learn
of the divine recognition of this distinction.

1. There is membership in the body of Christ corresponding to presence in the Kingdom of God. This takes in all who are Christ's, whether of any visible community or not. The Church in this sense is spoken of as the "body of Christ," and is also often called in these times the invisible Church. It may more properly be called the spiritual or general Church, because it includes all who are in the Kingdom of God's grace. Such Scriptures as the following give us this view of the Church: Eph. 3. 10. " To the intent that now unto the principalities and powers in heavenly places might be known by the church the manifold wisdom of God. * * * For this cause I bow my knees unto the Father of our Lord Jesus Christ, of whom the whole family in heaven and earth is named. * * * Unto him be glory in the church by Christ Jesus throughout all ages, world without end. Amen." Eph. 5. 23. " For the husband is the head of the wife, even as Christ is the head of the church ; and he is the saviour of the body. Therefore as the church is subject unto Christ, so let the wives be unto their own husbands in everything. Husbands, love your wives, even as Christ also loved the church, and gave himself for it, that he might present it to himself a glorious church, not having spot, or wrinkle, or any such thing ; but that it should be holy and without blemish. For no man ever yet hated his own flesh, but nourisheth and cherisheth it, even as the Lord the church ; for we are members of his body, of his flesh, and of his bones." Col. 1.

18. "And he is the head of the body, the church." Col. 1. 24, "Who now rejoice in my sufferings for you, and fill up that which is behind of the afflictions of Christ in my flesh for his body's sake, which is the church."

Now, in all these passages the inward and spiritual state is the basis of the idea of the Church. Those who are of His body are His Church; and they are of His Church who are subject to Christ—who are holy and without blemish. Let there be union with Christ and there is membership with this Church. This Church corresponds with the Kingdom of God, mentioned by Christ, Matt. 5. 20, "For I say unto you, that except your righteousness shall exceed the righteousness of the Scribes and Pharisees, ye shall in no case enter into the kingdom of heaven," and John 3. 3, "Except a man be born again he cannot see the kingdom of God," or by Paul, Rom. 14. 17, "For the kingdom of God is not meat and drink, but righteousness, and peace, and joy in the Holy Ghost," and also in Col. 1. 13, "Who hath delivered us from the power of darkness, and hath translated us into the kingdom of his dear Son."

It were useless to quote more at length on this point. We have given these for illustration sake, as well as for proof, of a very important point, that, though it is seldom denied, is nevertheless ignored. They show the universal Church of God as the "body of Christ,"—as "the kingdom of God—the kingdom of heaven." And in whatever of these different

descriptions it is presented to us, the spiritual state—
the divine work—is the essential thing. Whether the
subject be known to others or not he is still of
Christ's body, nay, "of his flesh and of his bones."
He needs no recognition from any others, whatever
position they may hold; nor is he introduced into this
state by the act of any. Is he "delivered from the
power of darkness and translated into the kingdom
of God's dear Son," then is he of this Church, which
Christ has "purchased with his own blood?" No
baptism of water is so much as mentioned; the
baptism of the Spirit is the initiating and the constituting act, by which he is introduced into the
kingdom of God.

To any one who has fully apprehended this divine
plan of constituting the children of men heirs to the
kingdom of heaven, it is almost an insult to urge any
argument against an act of man having any force in
such a work. And yet men have thought that the
keys to the kingdom of heaven were held by those
who had the right to administer water baptism.
They have, without any evidence, *assumed* what
ought to be very clearly proved, viz., that these
particular persons only, hold the right to baptize by
water; and that water baptism initiates a man into
the invisible Church of God.

But does God make the salvation of one man de-
pendent upon the will and act of another, so much,
that one can actually keep his fellow out of the
kingdom of God? Does God make Himself de-

pendent upon the offices of any man as to the
bestowment of His grace ? Our enlightened reason
can answer. " The Kingdom of God is not meat and
drink, but righteousness, and peace, and joy in the
Holy Ghost." " For in Jesus Christ neither circumcision availeth anything, nor uncircumcision, but
faith which worketh by love." I take it that neither
man nor child is any more a child of God, or a subject
of the kingdom of heaven, because of having been
baptized by water. It is a mistaken notion of the
nature of water baptism to assume the opposite of
this. Such a view would make it a saving ordinance ;
and in all who hold it, there is the tendency to
ceremonialism, and priestly claims, whether with
Anglican or Wesleyan.

Children without baptism may all be included as
in this Church or kingdom—whether we believe in
the doctrine of an actual spiritual life imparted, or of
covenant blessings unconditionally preventing damna-
tion, save for personal sins. Let none hold up their
hands in holy horror, as if the Church of God in this
sense were being desecrated by the presence of the
unbaptized. Wherever His covenant or His work of
grace has assured any of His favor, there are found
His members. And of them we need not be ashamed,
as He is not. In regard to their recognition as
members of the visible Church, I think too much is
made of the question. But of the work of saving all
children to the Church, whether baptized or unbaptized, we can never over-estimate the importance.

The question of their membership in the Church, similar to the membership of adults, is too often put forward as the ground of the duty to care for them. But their claim in this particular may be recognized and met on the one basis as well as on the other. The reader of the New Testament will notice that this phase of the Church is not one of which anything is said, save such as relates to personal duty and privilege, and such as relates to the divine work. It has nothing said of it, as of an organization in which man could act. There is another form of Church membership mentioned in the New Testament, viz. :

2. The Membership of the Local or Visible Community.

This is the Church which is mostly mentioned in the Acts of the Apostles. It should correspond, so far as it extends, with the invisible Church. But the latter may extend much further than the local Church. They can never be made absolutely co-extensive. Nor is it necessary they should. None should be admitted into the visible who are not of the invisible Church. None, it is supposed, will seek admission till they are of the Kingdom of God. And the Church is not wilfully to tolerate within its pale those who neither are, nor earnestly desire and seek to be members of Christ's body. Many may be truly of the Kingdom of God and heirs of heaven who are not in this local or visible Church. As distance or some other physical cause may hinder some true Christians from this membership, so incapacity may hinder others.

The student of the New Testament will notice that in regard to the local Church there is no very precise law laid down. Whether children of believers, for instance, were recognized members, as much as their parents, is not a subject that is discussed. Even Bushnell's attempt to prove that they are; by showing that in some of the Epistles they are personally addressed as to their duty, does not establish it. As well might we assume that all others who are addressed or appealed to, are members of the visible Church. Paul says to some, "Be ye reconciled to God," just as truly as he says, "Children, obey your parents." Indeed, much that is in the epistles is addressed to those who are not Christians; while each epistle as a whole is addressed to a local Church. The visible Church is not accounted the same as the saved world—nor as the baptized world. And most, if not all, the statements regarding the Church in the Acts of the Apostles, relate simply to the recognized Christian community, whose members personally participate in its privileges and duties, just as our modern discussion of Church membership must and should relate to those who personally can or do partake of its duties and privileges.

The local Church of the New Testament is the Church with which laws and discipline have to deal. And it is the Church in this sense that now corresponds to these local Churches of the New Testament, about which all ecclesiastical assemblies have to deal, and for which they are to legislate "according to the rule and doctrine of Christ." We may "write up the people " in this sense ; but in the other sense God only knows them all, and it is both useless and presumptuous for man to attempt to regulate it. Any attempt to construct the visible Church so as to include in it as actual members and subject to its godly discipline all who are in the Kingdom of God, and therefore of the invisible Church of God, must prove a failure. Moreover it is needless. There is no obligation imposed by the head of the Church requiring such an act of comprehension. All that is necessary to know and keep in mind is that the visible Church, that can be subject to discipline, does not control inheritance in "the Kingdom of Christ and of God." All believers in partaking of the new life, having thereby a desire begotten in them for this union with Christ's members, will seek it, and are obliged to have it. Visible Church membership will, then, according to these laws, include all who can be subject to the discipline of the Church, and all who can contribute to its edification—to its life and progress.

Such a doctrine and practice regarding the Church, will correspond exactly to the Word of God, in all that it says respecting the duty of the Church and its relation to the world. Turn unto the testimony of the New Testament upon this subject. Christ on two separate occasions mentions the Church. The first was, when in reply to Peter's confession, " Thou art the Christ, the Son of the living God," He said, " Upon this rock I will build my Church." Here he refers to

B

His Church in its most comprehensive sense, including the visible and the invisible. The other occasion is in regard to the offending brother: Matt. 18. 15, 16, 17, "Moreover, if thy brother trespass against thee, go and tell him his fault between thee and him alone: if he hear thee, then thou hast gained thy brother. But if he will not hear thee, then take with thee one or two more, that in the mouth of two or three witnesses every word may be established. And if he neglect to hear them, tell it unto the church; but if he neglect to hear the church, let him be unto thee as a heathen man and a publican.'' Here it is a visible community, and one that can take cognizance of what each of the parties has done. Whether it included any who would be unable to take due notice of the act, such as children for instance, is not fully established; but the natural construction of the terms leads to the conclusion that it did not. But the question is not left to be settled by this alone. The first mention of the Church in the Acts of the Apostles is in Chap. 2. 47, "And the Lord added unto the church daily such as should be saved." The visible Church of the New Testament was then in its formative state. It was little better than in embryo. The reading of the Revised Version is expository of this view: "And the Lord added to them day by day those that were being saved." The Church was made by drawing or uniting together those that were saved.

The idea of community is that which first finds

expression in the early days : "They went to their own company." "The multitudes of them that believed were of one heart and of one soul." The organized society comes afterward, and in the same way as would naturally come now in any analogous case. Men of similar minds, sympathies, and purposes naturally coalesce. The visible community soon comes to be spoken of as the Church. Acts 5. 11, "Great fear came upon all the church." Acts 8. 1, " At that time there was great persecution against the church which was at Jerusalem,"—a sort of intimation that there might be a Church elsewhere ; and so it really happens. Acts 9. 31, " Then had the churches rest throughout all Judea and Galilee." Already a number of local, visible Churches—simply companies of believers, who according to the Revised Version are "*the Church*." Its reading is, " So the *church* throughout all Judea and Galilee and Samaria had peace, being edified." Acts 11. 22, mention is again made of the Church which was at Jerusalem. They heard of the spread of the Gospel to Antioch and of a company of brethren there ; so they sent Barnabas. He went, and soon after brought Saul from Tarsus ; " And it came to pass that a whole year they as- sembled themselves with the church and taught much people, and the disciples were called Christians first in Antioch." The disciples are the Christians, and the Christians are the Church there. This com- munity of believers at Antioch is again mentioned in the 13th chap., 1st verse, as a Church, where Paul and

Barnabas were designated by the Holy Ghost for the work of God, as evangelists. Being separated by the Church for this purpose they begin a tour of missionary labor in preaching the Gospel far and wide. On completing it, they returned "to Lystra, and to Iconium, and Antioch," "confirming the souls of the disciples." Acts 13. 23, "And when they had ordained them elders in every church, and had prayed with fasting, they commended them to the Lord on whom they believed." Here is still the same idea of the visible Church—"the disciples," "the believers;" and here we have the development of the organized community or Church. Elders are appointed. In Paul's charge to the elders of Ephesus, Acts 20. 28, we have a fuller recognition of the organized Church, "Take heed, therefore, unto yourselves, and to all the flock over which the Holy Ghost hath made you overseers, to feed the church of God which he hath purchased with His own blood."

These instances might be still more extended ; but they are sufficient from the historical part of the New Testament. It is to be noticed that they all are local Churches, composed of actual believers—members who could perform the acts attributed to them. Perhaps two or three times these different Churches combined are called *the Church*—the visible, general Church.

Passing now to the Epistles, we find there the recognition of the local community, and the giving of rules to guide them as such. In the First Epistle to the Cor-

inthians, there is extended discussion of certain phases
of the Church's duty that gives much light on this
subject, of what is the visible Church—or whether the
Church is to be understood in any other sense than of
all who are in the Kingdom of God. 1 Cor. 14. 4, 5.
" He that speaketh in an unknown tongue, edifieth
himself ; but he that prophesieth, edifieth the Church."
"I would that ye all spake with tongues, but rather that
ye prophesied ; for greater is he that prophesieth than
he that speaketh with tongues, except he interpret,
that the church may receive edifying." It is an assembly that can be profited by discourse on the things
of God, and it is so made up that it is desirable that
all could speak with tongues, and still more that they
could " prophesy." We shall have occasion to turn to
this extended discussion of Paul again on another point
of still greater importance.

We need not mention other cases to show this idea of
the Church ; but this somewhat extended presentation
of the case is given because of its importance, and because it is indicative of the fact of the frequent—nay
general—mention of the Church in this sense of local and
visible. We thus see that membership in the Church,
which is a subject of discipline and of human man-
agement under divine law, is identification with a
community of disciples of Christ, as they are drawn
together by their common faith and love. It is secured
by the voluntary act of the individual when he becomes partaker of Christ. No initiation by any ceremony was necessary. Active participation in the

duties and privileges of a common brotherhood gave any one status in this community called a Church. But such was the nature of the community, that only saved ones would seek it, or could fulfil its duties.

We thus far in this connection state the nature of New Testament Church Membership. To go further, would be to anticipate the second point of enquiry. If in any way, those who are members of the Kingdom of God, while they are incapable of open participation ordinarily in its duties and privileges, as children, are members of this local community, it is not in such sense as in any way to affect the conditions of the membership of those of whom alone these records speak, and of whom extended discussion is made in the first Epistle to the Corinthians.

CHAPTER II.

THE CONDITIONS OF MEMBERSHIP.

What were the Conditions of this Local Church Membership?

IT is to be noted that only in the visible or local Church membership can we take account of these conditions. For whatever are the conditions upon which men enter into the kingdom of God, these are the conditions upon which they enter the spiritual, invisible, or universal Church. Membership in the invisible Church is not under the control of man, and he can appoint no regulations in regard to it. But membership in the visible Church is more within the reach of man; yet it is not a thing that man is to regulate, save in harmony with the Divine plan. The practice of the apostles, as given in the history of the Church recorded in the New Testament, must be the guide of the Church now. Yet even there is found no very explicit rules, but rather great principles are presented. The Church of the present has no right to demand any conditions contrary to the practice of the apostles, nor should they demand any less. The visible Church should still be the best and nearest approach to that kingdom in which Christ reigns, that is to be found in this world.

1. While a certain amount of religious knowledge and acceptance of certain doctrines were necessary, yet knowledge and orthodoxy were not conditions of membership in the Church of the New Testament. No such thing as an examination in regard to either of these points, is so much as once hinted at in any part of the record. Only as these could and did affect the desires and character of any person, did they come into consideration. Only as men knew the truth as it is in Jesus, could they earnestly desire to be saved. There would be no attempt to turn from sin until they saw its hatefulness, and there would be no turning to Christ as the Saviour of sinners until they believed Him to be the only Saviour. The saving, or, at least, the awakening process, must in the nature of the thing precede the question of Church membership. As well

might we expect to see a community of savages joining
in an organization to promote the circulation of a
newspaper, as to expect sinful and unawakened men to
join together in christian fellowship. The law of desire,
if not of demand, is the controlling rule in this matter.
The truth proclaimed, constrains men to cry out, " Men
and brethren, what shall we do ? " They are told to
believe on the Lord Jesus Christ, and doing so, there
springs up in them a desire for closer communion with
all who have in like manner fled to Christ for refuge.
This becomes the basis of their relation to the community of disciples,—to the Church.

To thus believe, in order to such result, there must
be a certain amount of religious truth accepted, and to
this degree this knowledge and correct view of truth
becomes a condition of their connection with the visible
Church. The test, however, is not applied at the point
of their seeking association with the disciples, but as
a condition of receiving such spiritual quickening as
produces the desire for this relation to the Church.
There is no application of this rule in such a case.
Desire for, or attainment of the thing that draws
together the christian community, precedes all consideration of the outward relationship. This secret divine
power is the essential thing in the kingdom of God.
It is the great need of man and of the race.

This is the natural and the divine order. Cornelius
seeks the knowledge of salvation by faith in Christ
and the gift of the Holy Ghost, before any question of
his relation to the visible Church is so much as hinted

at. Lydia and the jailer at Phillippi are both con-
verted before Church membership is apparently so much
as thought of. The new converts at Antioch are visited
by Barnabas for their spiritual edification, not to or-
ganize them into a Church. So when Peter and John
went down to Samaria, after Philip had preached unto
them, and they had believed and were baptized, their
enquiry was not even whether the Church had been
organized, or what was their faith or knowledge, but
they "prayed for them, that they might receive the
Holy Ghost, for as yet he was fallen upon none of
them." Their concern was that these people should be
true christians, that they should have that which is the
true and essential characteristic of disciples, the Holy
Ghost.

And that which is characteristic of these cases is
equally characteristic of the establishment of every
Church mentioned in the New Testament. The cause
and condition of their organization, or of individual
membership, is not knowledge or orthodoxy, but the
possession of that spiritual gift which draws them all
to each other around the common centre, Christ. The
Rev. William Arthur, in his "Tongue of Fire," says,
" Christianity was established by the creation of
christians." In like manner it may be said the
Churches were organized by the creation of christians.

2. Neither was baptism a condition of New Testament Church membership. I have reference in this
case to the initiation into membership in the visible
Church. Baptism is an obligation of the christian

religion, and cannot be neglected without commission of an act that is just ground of exclusion from the Church of God. But the same may be said of the Lord's Supper. It also is a plain duty of every Christian, and he who neglects this duty is also worthy of exclusion. Much more than this has been claimed for baptism. It has been assumed that it is an initiating act into the visible Church, so that only such as are baptized are admitted to be members of the visible Church. Some can see but little importance in baptism except in this view of the case. This view we believe to be unwarranted, if not mischievous. That baptism was usually administered soon after conversion I readily admit. But so also the Lord's Supper was received very soon after conversion. And strong presumptive evidence exists that it was often received before baptism was administered; for as the Lord's Supper seems to have been received at every assembly of the disciples there was probably opportunity to receive it before baptism could have been administered. *It* might, therefore, be regarded as an initiatory rite just as fairly as baptism. So far as I can see this position has been assumed without any definite proof. It is not our business to prove the negative. It is sufficient to say, there is no evidence that water baptism initiates any one into the visible Church.

In view of the absence of any intimation in the New Testament that it was initiatory—and therefore necessary to membership—its early recognition as initiatory must reasonably be regarded as one of those unhappy tendencies to ceremonialism that early showed themselves in the Church.

A convert might receive baptism and then positively refuse to take membership in the visible Church. And there can be no visible Church membership without the person's own consent and act. It is a recognition of what already exists—of his introduction into the kingdom of God, or of his sincere desire and endeavor to enter that kingdom. This idea is in harmony with the teaching of the Church standards on this point; but the idea of initiatory rite into the visible Church, upon which much stress has of late years been laid, is not taught there. Nor is it implied in the nature of the act. As circumcision was a sign and seal of the righteousness had by him who received it, so water baptism is a sign and seal of the covenant blessings enjoyed or pledged. The reception of water baptism stood in no immediate or necessary relation to reception into the visible Church. That which fitted the character and disposed the will to seek it, and also union with God's people, secured membership without any external rite. I dwell upon it here because it has been assumed that every baptized person, and such only, was a member of the visible Church. This places water baptism where the Scriptures, as I conceive, do not put it. And from this position it has been urged that baptized children are members of the visible Church, and that great in_justice is done them if this membership is denied them.

Perhaps the error arises from misconception of what is meant by *membership in the visible or local Church*. The analogy of the Jewish Church, corresponding with the Jewish nation, does not uphold this claim. And the analogy does not exist. They may be regarded as members of the invisible Church, whether baptized or not; and if we change the meaning of visible Church they may, as children of parents in the visible Church, be regarded as members also. But in such case we do not mean a Church of active members who can exercise discipline and be subject to it; who can each participate in its privileges and perform the common duties of actual members. This we think must be accepted as the sense of Church in the New Testament, unless where it refers to the invisible Church. Then this "body of Christ" includes children even unbaptized. The baptism is a recognition of their standing and their claims to christian nurture. This sense of the local and visible Church is the one prevalent and underlying all modern ecclesiastical legislation. On no well established basis, therefore, can the question of the relation of baptized or unbaptized children to the visible Church, affect the nature or duties of visible Church membership in general, or of the conditions upon which it is acquired or retained.   .

All the proper christian instincts of parents, and all the historic Jewish identification of children with their parents in covenant privileges, are fully met by their recognition as rightly partakers of water baptism, because they are in the kingdom of God or the universal Church, have the covenant of God in full force for them, and have a right to the sign and seal of this covenant. And all the duties of parents and of the Church can also as fully be performed with this conception of their relation, as with that which regards them as full members of the visible and local Church. It is not a question of the amount of care that the Church shall bestow upon them, nor of their present gracious relation—whatever that may be.

Nor is it the question how the transition of an irresponsible child from the position he holds in the invisible Church, to actual, voluntary and responsible membership in the visible Church, shall be secured. It is: How does the New Testament show that a responsible man entered the visible Church? We hold it was not on the ground of his correct acceptance of doctrine, nor the extent of his knowledge, nor by his receiving baptism. And we might add it was not by virtue of his having been in the invisible Church in childhood, or in the *visible* Church in childhood, nor by virtue of his baptism and his parents' choice, as some in these times teach, is to be his right now. Neither orthodoxy, nor knowledge, nor rites, nor childhood's privileges, nor parental choice or grace gave membership in the visible Church of the New Testament.

Perhaps some classes of enquirers on this subject, particularly those who have very strong tendencies to hierarchical views, will be surprised at the absence of technical rules. But it is in harmony with the entire drift of the new dispensation to exalt only the essentials. How then did men become members of this new community?

3. They became members of the Church by being led, under the direct work of God in them, creating spiritual desires, purposes, and life, to ally themselves with the community of the disciples. Let a man, whether Jew or Gentile, under the power of the Gospel, however it may have been preached to him, see his sinfulness and need of salvation, and let him as a consequence seek the assembly of the disciples for aid, and there find the Saviour; that man has passed the door of the visible Church. He has become a christian in heart and by profession; and by continuing to join with them in their assemblies in order to build up himself and his brethren in the faith, becomes a member of the Church. It is not by solemn and stately ceremony, but by a divine power making a new life, and thus causing a new alliance.

Many things may enter into the means of his attaining such a position, and still others of great importance exist as conditions of his continuing to hold it. These we shall presently consider at length, because they enter equally into the question we have in hand. But in the meantime the one act which gives him this position of membership is that complex act of his seeking it in the state of mind here described, and their acceptance of him under the persuasion that he is one with them in the possession of the same experience of the power of Christ to save. He and they might possibly be deceived, though that is very improbable, but in the meantime he is a member of the visible Church. But if he is deceived he is not a member of the invisible Church. They may baptize him and still he is not. They may admit him to that Holy Supper and still he is not introduced into the kingdom of God. But believing him truly a believer they give him the badge of discipleship— baptism ; and on his continuing to fulfil the conditions of discipleship they will give him continued recognition of their brotherhood, in the Lord's Supper, of which he must partake as a duty and a privilege.

Around this point really gather the varied conditions of continued Church membership. Participation of the Lord's Supper with the christian brotherhood is the common duty of the Church, and in order that it may rightly be received, the christian life must be lived, and the christian fellowship must be maintained.

In these two things we have the main conditions and characteristics of New Testament Church membership.

4. There must be the practice of the christian life. "If ye love me keep my commandments," says the Great Teacher. The Church is His fold into which He gathers His people, and they who enter are under obligation to obey His law. Whatever the christian life requires, that they are bound to fulfil. Paul commands the membership of the Church at Thessa-

lonica to "withdraw yourselves from every brother
that walketh disorderly and not after the tradition
which he received of us." And he further says, " If
any man obey not our word by this epistle, note that
man and have no company with him that he may be
ashamed. Yet count him not as an enemy but ad-
monish him as a brother." " Mark them which cause
divisions and offences contrary to the doctrine which
ye have learned, and avoid them." " I have written
unto you not to keep company, if any man that is
called a brother be a fornicator, or covetous, or an
idolator, or a railer, or a drunkard, or an extortioner,
with such an one, no, not to eat." Thus, we see that
the law of Christ was enforced to the extent of for-
bidding to eat the Lord's Supper with such sinners as
are here mentioned. Expulsion was required to be
used against those who transgressed the divine rule.

But, perhaps, it will be urged that this expulsion
was to be used only against such as committed some
specific crime, and that, therefore, a man might rightly
remain in the Church while he did not do these things,
though, perhaps, he did not really serve God and live
the Christian life. There may possibly be a distinction
drawn between what is actually required of all members in the Church, and what acts are mentioned as
those, demanding direct Church discipline ; because we
may be able accurately to determine whether some
acts are really performed, and whether these can be
done by a Christian, while in the case of others we
may not be able to determine them. But it does not

follow, therefore, that only such acts are to be shunned as are of this open kind, and which so distinctly prove the lack of the christian character. Nor is it by any means to be assumed that only a negative goodness is required as a condition of Church membership, any more than it is for christian life. The positive side of christian life is enjoined as a condition of this position, though we may not be able to discern its absence so clearly as to be able to make it a cause of excommunication. "If any man love not the Lord Jesus Christ let him be anathema maranatha," is said in immediate connection with a discussion on this very subject of the exercise of christian discipline. The obligations to live religion, as binding on the individual member of the Church, are obligations that the Church has a right to require of its members. How it can enforce the obligation is solved only by remembering the next condition of Church membership, which we are soon to discuss, viz : his obligation to participate in christian fellowship in the christian assembly. Its application makes the individual member an unconscious judge of himself, as far as such is possible, and it also places all his fellow-members in a position to know, with considerable accurateness, even this deep secret of his heart.

No institution or rule that has to be worked or administered by man, can be absolutely correct in its operations. The Church may sometimes have within its fold a member who is not a true christian, who passes undetected. But the application of these two

C

rules guards against this danger, so far as fallible
man can guard the point. And beyond this it is to be
kept in mind, that whether these are efficient methods
or not, still the condition of membership holds the
same, whether we can so apply the rule as to detect
every departure from it or not.

If the Epistles are addressed to the Churches, and
set forth what religion is, and what christians are to
be, then, whatever they require is really a condition of
membership in the visible Church. The individual
member is in duty bound to apply the rule to his own
conscience and life. They assume the personal
sincerity of all who are addressed, and set forth what
they are to be. The christian life is the life to be
lived by the Church. It exists for the purpose of
aiding all who desire to live it, and it is only when
men desire to live for God that they will seek its fold.
Their presence here is a profession that they are de-
siring and striving to be christians; and if they are
in the visible Church without understanding themselves as thus committed to Christ's service, then they
are inexcusably ignorant of its nature or guilty of
prostituting the Church of God to unworthy purposes.
It is a divine institution set up on earth to raise man
to heaven. The man who is in it, and makes no
earnest attempts to keep Christ's law, violates the
very first principles of an institution, of which He is
a member.

It has sometimes been said that the Methodist
Church required attendance at its select Church

meeting, and yet did not demand a christian life.
The statement is very far from the truth, and is made
because those who utter it do not discriminate very
closely in regard to things that differ. The same
might be said on just as good ground, without very
much variation, even in the terminology, in regard to
the Church membership of the New Testament. It
prescribes expulsion for specific sins, and yet does not
prescribe expulsion for absence of piety. In giving
the privileges of the Lord's Supper only to such as
attend its very select christian assembly, it expels for
non-attendance on these means, and yet it does not
prescribe expulsion for neglect of personal prayer.
But the reason is upon the face of it, and the teaching of the Scriptures need mislead nobody. There are
things which man cannot judge, and here man is not
enjoined to judge. There are things that man's own
conduct in regard to them may be taken as a test of
his position on the subject, and so the rule may be
applied on his own action. This is precisely how the
application of the conditions of Church membership
in the Methodist Church stands; and these are the
principles that are presented in the New Testament as
regulating the christian community. The whole of
the christian life is required. Where our fellow-
disciples can judge they are authorized to judge; and
where they cannot judge, we are placed in a position
where we almost unconsciously judge ourselves.
Within these lines, I am not aware that any provision is made against insincerity. That must be

mainly the ground where the "tares" will grow
with the wheat until harvest, when the Great
Searcher of hearts will "try every man's work of
what sort it is."

In order to this Church membership.

5. There must be fellowship in the christian assembly, and observance of Christian ordinances.

This comes as a natural result; as a necessary
means of spiritual growth, and as a condition of observance of the divine commandment, "Do this in
remembrance of me."

It is a natural result. These early christians loved
one another. This love bound them together. A
common faith, a common aim, a common experience
resulted in the closest union. The history of the
early days and years of the work of God in apostolic
times shows that they were a most perfect brotherhood. Partakers of one spirit, and subjects of one
common Master, they naturally sought each other's
society. They were surrounded by one common foe,
and committed to one common work, which made it
desirable to aid each other. Their experience of
divine things was not only new but wonderful, so as
to lead them to desire to speak to each other on the
subject. And with minds renewed they delighted in
this holy converse more than in any other exercises.
Love one to another was a main characteristic of the
disciples of Christ then. It is so still, and must remain the same to the end of time. The world were
strangers to their new experience. Their joys and

hopes were known only to themselves ; and were too
thrilling to be kept covered up in the secret of their
own hearts.

Everything pertaining to them and their relation to
the world outside, as well as the command and design
of their divine Lord, made it most natural for them to
assemble together statedly for mutual edification.

It was a necessary means of spiritual growth.
They needed spiritual strengthening, that they might
be able to war a good warfare. The nature of man
and the nature of religion alike, make it a necessity
that believers should fellowship together. They must
have gatherings for mutual edification. No christian
will make progress, such as he should, when he is
isolated from the brotherhood of believers. If his
circumstances are providentially appointed so that he
is debarred the fellowship of saints, he may possibly
continue to grow up into Christ, his living head, in all
things; but he will much need the assembly of God's
saints. God has appointed it for his spiritual growth,
and all the instincts of his renewed nature will lead
him to seek it. He can most truly say, " I was glad
when they said unto me, let us go up into the house
of the Lord. There they " bear one another's burdens;"
there they " provoke one another unto love and good
works." The fainting are revived, the wandering are
brought back, the ignorant are instructed, and the
sorrowful are made glad. The feet that had " well
nigh slipped " are placed securely on the rock again,
by their gathering together in His name, and the ful-

filment of His promise. "there am I in the midst of
them." Fellowship with God, in the assembly of His
saints, builds them up in their most holy faith. "They
go from strength to strength ; every one of them in
Zion appeareth before God."

This assembling with the brotherhood of the disciples is in obedience to the divine will, and necessary
to a full observance of all divine ordinances. Herein
it becomes a condition of New Testament Church
membership.

The obligation to assemble with the disciples in
their gatherings for mutual edification may be established by three classes of evidence. (a) From
express command. Hebrews 10. 24, 25, "And let us
consider one another, to provoke unto love and good
works : not forsaking the assembling of ourselves
together, as the manner of some is, but exhorting one
another ; and so much the more as ye see the day
approaching." This was the Church law which they
had to keep. (b) From the approved practice of
the early disciples. This is so common and undoubted a fact in the record of the New Testament
that it is scarcely necessary to cite instances. A
few must suffice.

The cases at the same time show the nature of
these assemblies.

Beginning with Acts 2. 42, "And they continued
steadfastly in the apostle's doctrine and fellowship
and in breaking of bread, and in prayers." Here is
implied or stated the things that were done, and thus,

the nature of the meetings of the disciples is un-folded. In the 4th chapter of Acts, 23rd verse, the christian assembly is again mentioned, "And, being let go, they went to their own company, and reported all that the chief priests and elders had done unto them, and when they heard that, they lifted up their voice with one accord," etc. At 31st verse of same chapter it is recorded, "And when they had prayed they were all filled with the Holy Ghost." In the 5th chapter further mention is made of their assembly, "And they were all with one accord in Solomon's porch, and of the rest durst no man join himself to them; but the people magnified them." Acts 14. 27, "And when they were come, and had gathered the Church together, they rehearsed all that God had done with them, and how he had opened the door of faith unto the Gentiles." Acts 15. 30, "So when they were dismissed they came to Antioch, and when they had gathered the multitude together they delivered the epistle, which, when they had read, they rejoiced for the consolation. And Judas and Silas being prophets also themselves, exhorted the brethren with many words, and confirmed them." In Acts 20. 7, we have still more specific intimation, not only of an act but of a practice. "And upon the first day of the week when the disciples came together to break bread, Paul preached unto them, ready to depart on the morrow." The regularity of their practice forces itself upon any reader of the New Testament.

The obligation to attend these assemblies of the disciples is also proved from—

(c) The administration of the Lord's Supper being performed only in such assemblies ; and yet all were under divine law to participate in this feast. The lengthened discussion on this subject in 1 Corinthians, to which we shall soon refer, is sufficent proof of this position.

If then, there was command to assemble, and the practice of assembling, and also participation of the Lord's Supper in such assembly, it is beyond question that the members of the Church in New Testament times were under obligation, one and all, to meet with their brethren in their assemblies.

For greater distinctness, we will consider the other part of this general question in a separate chapter.

CHAPTER III.

THE CHARACTER AND WORK OF THESE ASSEMBLIES

What was the Character and Work of these Meetings of the New Testament Church ?

THIS is a most important enquiry ; for upon the answer depends the conclusion at which this discussion aims.

We take it that the instances already cited and those yet to be produced, show that these meetings were select christian assemblies, and not promiscuous gatherings ; that they were for mutual edification, and christian discipline ; that the exercises of prayer,

praise, exhortation, prophesying, statement of christian experience, reproving, comforting, and instruc-
ting, were mutually participated in ; and that the
celebration of the Lord's Supper was there performed.

In addition to the evidence which the history of the
Church, as given in the Acts of the Apostles affords,
we have still more direct testimony to the points
above stated, in the epistles to the Churches. The
exclusive christian character of the meetings for
mutual edification, for discipline, and for participation
in the Lord's Supper, is made abundantly clear in
Paul's First Epistle to Corinthians v. 4–11 : "In the
name of our Lord Jesus Christ, when ye are gathered
together, and my spirit, with the power of our Lord
Jesus Christ, to deliver such an one unto Satan for
the destruction of the flesh, that the spirit may be
saved in the day of the Lork Jesus. . . . . But
now I have written unto you not to keep company,
if any man that is called a brother, be a fornicator,
or covetous, or an idolator, or a railer, or a drunkard,
or an extortioner ; with such an one no, not to eat."
These words cannot refer to the christian in his social
life, but to the christian in the assembly ; and they
thus show in part the work done, the discipline required
to be observed, and the purity of the Church to be
maintained.

The same is apparent in the language of the
same epistle, xi. 17, 18 : "Now in this that I declare
unto you, I praise you not, that ye come together
not for the better, but for the worse. For, first of all,

when ye come together in the church, I hear that there are divisions among you." In the fourth verse preceding, the statement more fully indicates the exercises and the extent of participation in those exercises : "Every man praying or prophesying having his head covered dishonoureth his head. But every woman that prayeth or prophesieth with her head uncovered dishonoureth her head." This rule evidently was designed for a meeting, rather than for privacy. The whole chapter unfolds the nature of these gatherings. Prophesying, and that even by the women, was a part; the exercise of discipline even to the extent of exclusion of an unworthy brother, was allowable and enjoined. To avoid what was unseemly they are enjoined to examine themselves, and thus save the necessity of being judged by others.

The twelfth chapter of this epistle is a still further unfolding of the nature of the Church and the relation of one member to another. Different gifts were bestowed on different persons in the body of Christ— the Church—but all by the same Spirit. And special stress is laid upon the point that all these were to be used for the edification of the Church. "Whether one member suffer all the members suffer with it ; or one member be honoured all the members rejoice with it. Now ye are the body of Christ, and members in particular." This may be taken as a sort of key to the whole discussion.

Then, in the thirteenth chapter, follows his eulogy on charity; after which he begins his statement of

rules that should govern the disciples in their meetings for the edification of each other. Looking at
these we get a pretty clear insight into the style and
character of the christian assembly of the apostolic
times. " Follow after charity, and desire spiritual gifts,
but rather that ye may prophesy. . . But he that
prophesieth speaketh unto men to edification and exhortation and comfort. He that speaketh in an unknown tongue edifieth himself, but he that prophesieth edifieth the Church." The edification of the
Church is to be the main object aimed at. Believers
are to be built up in their most holy faith. This is
the object of their assembling ; this is the intense
desire of their hearts. Their inward spiritual life is
to be made strong and pure, and their outward walk
is to be so governed that it shall be irreproachable.
All the gifts and graces bestowed on the individual
members of the Church are to be used for the good
of all. " Even so ye, forasmuch as ye are zealous of
spiritual gifts, seek that ye may excel to the edifying
of the Church." . , . " Tongues are for a sign,
not to them that believe, but to them that believe
not ; but prophesying serveth not for them that believe not, but for them that believe. If, therefore,
the whole Church be come together into one place
and all speak with tongues, and there come in those
that are unlearned or unbelievers, will they not say
that ye are mad. But if all prophesy and there come
in one that believeth not or one unlearned, he is con-
vinced of all, he is judged of all. And thus are the

secrets of his heart made manifest; and so **falling**
down on his face he will worship God, and report that
God is in you of a truth."

Much more in harmony with these statements might
be given, but we turn now to other epistles.   And
here we find the same uniform testimony of the nature
of the Church, and of the Church assembly, of the
object of its gathering, the means of its accomplishing
this object; and of its particular duties. Ephesians iv.
16: "From whom the whole body fitly joined together
and compacted, by that which every joint supplyeth
according to the effectual working in the measure of
every part, maketh increase of the body unto the
edifying of itself in love." Under the figure of a
body we have the nature of the Church relationship
and the mutual duty of its members. Ephesians v.
11, 19: "And have no fellowship with the unfruitful
works of darkness, but rather reprove them." But
they are to attend to the very opposite, for they
have been awakened from the sleep of sin and death.
"And be not drunk with wine, wherein is excess, but
be filled with the Spirit; speaking to yourselves in
psalms and hymns, and spiritual songs, singing and
making melody in your heart to the Lord; giving
thanks always for all things unto God and the Father
in the name of our Lord Jesus Christ; submitting
yourselves one to another in the fear of God."

Colossians iii. 16: "Let the word of Christ dwell
in you richly in all wisdom; teaching and admonishing one another in psalms and hymns, and spiritual

songs, singing with grace in your hearts to the
Lord."

Still more explicit is the language in Hebrews x.
24, 25: "And let us consider one another to provoke
unto love and good works; not forsaking the assembling of ourselves together as the manner of some is,
but exhorting one another; and so much the more as
ye see the day approaching."

All these reveal both a practice on the part of the
Church and a teaching on the part of the apostle in
harmony with the first record regarding the fellowship
of the Church in Acts ii. 42: "And they continued
steadfastly in the apostles' doctrine and fellowship,
and in breaking of bread and in prayers." The com-
ment of Rev. William Arthur in his "Tongue of
Fire," on this record is applicable in a considerable
degree to all these extended quotations on this subject,
"Besides breaking of bread, and doctrine, and prayers,
'fellowship' is distinctly named. It was then not a
Church where the teaching of the minister was taken
for his fellowship with the people, and their breaking
of bread for their fellowship one with another; but
where, in addition to public teaching, sacraments, and
prayers, was another beauty of primitive Christianity,
'fellowship.' Fellowship is family life, forming a
circle, smaller or larger, to the members of which joys,
sorrows, interests, and undertakings, are common
concern and matters of common conversation." Surely
no stronger evidence could be given to the point we
maintain.

If any analysis of all these portions of Holy Scripture was necessary it might be given. Their effect is to produce in the form of direct and yet cumulative testimony the following conclusions:—

1. That the first christians were in the habit of regularly meeting together for mutual edification.

2. That these meetings were under apostolic sanction, and were governed by instructions given under inspiration.

3. That they were made up not of a promiscuous assembly, but of avowed disciples.

4. That they had duties and privileges that did not permit the common presence of the worldly.

5. That in these meetings all might take part in the exercises, which consisted in prayer, prophesying, instruction, fellowship, judging in the case of one unworthy, partaking of the Lord's Supper, etc. And all for the edification of each other.

6. That attendance of the disciples at these meetings was expressly required by apostolic command and regulation.

If these are fair deductions from the Scriptures thus speaking on this subject—and that they are, no fair-minded person can deny,—then we see that the christian assembly, or Church meeting of the New Testament was not one gathered together to hear a solitary person preach the Gospel, and conduct the acts of praise and prayer all by his own act—such as our public religious services—but rather a gathering for mutual aid and encouragement, where all might

and were expected to take part. Where prayer, and
fellowship, and prophesying, and exhortation, were
common acts to be mutually participated in, and where
edification was ever the main design. All the elements
of public worship and of Church work were here
attended to.

And it is to be kept in mind that, while the obligation to attend is put beyond doubt, by apostolic practice, instruction, and command, such was the disposition
of the early christians that in general no particular
command was needed. Only where the duty was
being neglected does the express command appear.
The early disciples, by common consent arising out of
their new found life, joy, and aims, were constrained
to meet together. By this all men might know that
they were Christ's disciples, because they showed how
they loved one another. They had one life, one aim,
one common experience that drew them together in
mutual fellowship. The *grace was stronger than any
peculiarities of constitution or tastes;* so that with
unerring certainty every believer would love such
gatherings, and voluntarily seek their enjoyment.

Here they joined around one common table in
memory of Him whom they all loved, worshipped,
and obeyed. Nor is it conceivable that any man, with
such a heart, and with such regard to the rights of
others, as a Christian would have, would presume to
say " I will not associate with these people in their
meetings for prayer, and exhortation, and fellowship,
but I will claim my right to sit down with them to

the table of the Lord." And if there had arisen such
a strange mixture of piety and assurance, it is not at
all likely that these early christians, who were so
watchful over each other's welfare, and the purity of
the Church of God, would admit him to so high a
privilege. His demand would be unreasonable, and
the granting of it would be unsafe. He does not
show such evidence of genuine love to God, or the
brotherhood, or such concern for spiritual edification
as to warrant their recognizing him as a brother.

We may now direct attention to the point of enquiry for which the preceding has been preparatory.

CHAPTER IV.

AGREEMENT OF METHODIST CHURCH CONDITIONS.

*Are the Conditions of Membership in the Methodist
Church in Harmony with the Conditions of Membership in the Church in New Testament Times?*

WE have ascertained the conditions of New Testament Church membership. Let us see what are the
conditions of membership in the Methodist Church;
and then we can mark their agreement.

1. The Methodist Church does not require a
particular amount of religious knowledge, or agree_
ment with what she believes to be the doctrines of
Holy Scripture. She says to all, "There is only one

condition previously required of all who desire ad-mission into these societies, viz: a desire to flee from the wrath to come, and to be saved from their sins." The man may be very ignorant of religious doctrine in general, but if he desires to flee from the wrath to come, and be saved from his sins, she is ready to help him. This desire to flee from the wrath to come, and be saved from his sins, implies the knowledge of the fundamental doctrines of Christianity. He may hold much not in agreement with her standards of teaching, and yet, if a controlling desire to be saved dwells in him, he is not excluded. Her great aim is to save men —not to enforce doctrinal agreement.

2. If he is admitted on such condition it is further demanded that he should continue to evidence his desire for salvation, " *By doing no harm ; by avoid-ing evil of every kind.*" Here the life of the man comes under control, and he must abstain from sin. Any endeavour to teach that the Methodist Church may exclude for simple non-attendance on her select meetings—her class-meetings—and yet permit mem-bership to him who is living in sin, must be done in total ignorance of the terms of the "General Rules," or else by ignoring them. As every man who wants to be a christian must, in obedience to the New Testa-ment, abstain from sin, so every one who desires to be a Methodist must "avoid evil of every kind." The New Testament Church did not allow open trans-gressors within her communion; nor does the Method-ist Church permit it. Every such person in her

D

communion, is a rebel to her laws. The outward life, while not the main thing, must be kept in harmony with the inward life, which it is her great aim to promote. She teaches that there can be no communion with God, or indwelling spiritual life in him who lives in sin ; and accordingly she demands that he "cease from sin."

3. In addition to this negative obedience, great as it is, she requires him, in order to his continuance in her fold, "to do good of every possible sort." To do good to the bodies and souls of men ; "to instruct, reprove, and exhort all we have any intercourse with." Charity and zeal are to go hand in hand, and exert themselves to their utmost to do good to all.

The christian race is to be run ; and in order to it self-denial is to be practiced, and cross-bearing is to be performed. Endurance of trial for Christ's sake is to be accepted. The christian life, indeed, and truth must be entered on and practiced, or there is no compliance with the express rules of Methodism. It does not permit a base and careless worldliness to be characteristic of her subjects. Any such cases are violations of her laws and spirit, as they are antagonistic to the law and spirit of the New Testament.

4. The Methodist Church requires its members to attend "all the ordinances of God." She requires them to attend her most select and holy convocations —her class-meetings, or her meetings of professed disciples of Christ for mutual edification. Is this contrary to the law of the New Testament, or is it in agreement with it ?

We have seen what the nature of the New Testament Church meeting was : what were its exercises, and what the law of attendance was. Now, does this *Methodist Church meeting* which, perperhaps, unfortunately is called a *class-meeting*, differ materially from the meeting of the disciples as given in the New Testament ? And does the obligation to attend differ to such degree as to be material ? To both of these questions we think only a negative answer is possible.

(1) This Church meeting is made up of believers, or of those seeking to be such, and who voluntarily assemble for the purpose of helping each other "to work out their salvation." No more could be said of the meetings of the Church in the New Testament, so far as relates to the persons constituting them. They were not a promiscuous assembly. The Methodist Church meeting follows the same rule. They were drawn together by spiritual interests and influences. This is the professed object and the undoubted reason of the gathering of every class-meeting. Worldliness never voluntarily seeks its holy associations. They are appointed and conducted for the edification of believers. Nothing but spiritual interests concern them, or are sought to be promoted by them.

(2) These meetings are characterized by the same exercises as those which engaged the meetings of the early disciples. In these meetings God's people engage in prayer and praise, in christian fellow-

ship, in exhortation and admonition, in rejoicing
and comforting. They who know their exercises can
testify that they are a close carrying out of Paul's
command to the Collossians, " Let the word of Christ
dwell in you richly in all wisdom; teaching and
admonishing one another in psalms, and hymns, and
spiritual songs, singing with grace in your hearts to
the Lord." This is their spirit and aim, and this is, to
a large degree, their real character. Any failure in this
particular is not from their nature or design, but
simply from human imperfection. They are closely
conformed to the command of Paul to the Hebrews,
where he enjoins the use of similar meetings in the
New Testament Church : "And let us consider one
another to provoke unto love and good works, not forsaking the assembling of ourselves together, as the
manner of some is, but exhorting one another ; and so
much the more as ye see the day approaching."

The agreement of the class-meeting with the New
Testament Church meeting, extending this far, is
quite sufficient for our purpose. But it does not stop
here. The love-feast is but an extension of the class-
meeting—a combination of a number of classes together, but for the same purpose. And here the Lord's
Supper is administered to the members of these classes,
constituting the aggregate Church for that locality.
Still further; a member charged with crime is account-
able to his class, and subject to trial by it—provision
being made that it may be done by a select number of
them, for convenience sake, but carrying out the
principle all the same. This is also in agreement

with the law, as we have discovered it in the New
Testament. Throughout all this there is a marvellous
agreement, as if by design ; but really by an over-
ruling Providence. The idea of any disagreement
with either the principles of Church membership in
the New Testament, or of practices contrary to theirs,
finds no countenance from the facts.

(3) Nor does the law of attendance differ, any more
than these already mentioned particulars. To forsake
the assembly of the disciples in the Primitive Church
was to disobey apostolic command, and to proclaim
themselves as not of their community. Its neglect
shews a sad want of desire for spiritual edification·
No man could reasonably claim the Lord's Supper who
forsook the Church, nor would the Church grant its
privileges to one who placed himself beyond their
oversight. And the nature of the refusal would not
create in this respect any difficulty whatever. The
disposition to desire and seek ͺparticipation of the
Lord's Supper, and yet not to desire and seek christian
fellowship for edification, is indicative of the spirit of
formalism rather than of religious life and joy. The
man who would not desire Christian fellowship and
edification, would not, or should not, desire the Lord's
Supper. By his own act he excludes himself. Now,
in all this there is still a close following, both of the
spirit and the practice of the New Testament Church.
The neglector excludes himself, and upon this exclusion the Church can declare that he is no longer a
member of the Church. His own act has declared
what he desired.

The comparison we have thus presented between New Testament Church membership and Methodist Church membership shows such an agreement, not only with main principles, but even in the details as to prove, beyond the possibility of contradiction, that the rules of Church membership in the Methodist Church are thoroughly Scriptural. The conditions of admission and continuance are the same. The double mode of exclusion by trial or by voluntary act of neglect taken account of, are notably alike.

These views should not be regarded merely as the opinions of a partial advocate; because they are supported by a weight of evidence, as we have seen, that ought to be overwhelming. But let us have the testimony of one, not an upholder of this system. The learned Dr. Paley gives the following testimony on this subject, " After men became Christians much of their time was spent in prayer and devotion, in religious meetings, in celebrating the Eucharist, in conferences, in affectionate intercourse with one another, and correspondence with other societies. Perhaps their mode of life, in its form and habit, was not unlike the *Unitas Fratrum*, or the modern Methodist." And in these later years when some, as I think loose Methodists, are decrying the class or the obligation to attend it, a distinguished Congregational minister of England (Dr. Dale) said to the Wesleyan Methodist Conference there: " I have often said to my own friends that I heartily wished that we Congregationalists could somehow or other, transplant to our soil, what seemed to have flourished so luxuriantly in yours—I mean, sir, the class-meeting. * * It does appear to me that you have amongst you, that of which in some sort you are trustees. We hold you responsible for preserving in its entirety the essential principle and genius of this institution." Surely in view of such opinions and with the knowledge of its, great advantages to Methodism, and the spiritual feasts it has secured to those who have used it, all such ought to love it, and join heart and hand to uphold and preserve it as a God-given heritage.

CHAPTER V.

COLLATERAL EVIDENCE.

Let us Look at a few Collateral Considerations.

1. THESE methods of procedure, which are so Scriptural, are peculiarly adapted to the nature of the case, and the design for which the Church exists. If to build up "a chosen generation, a royal priesthood, an holy nation, a peculiar people;" that should show forth the praises of Him who hath called them, "out of darkness unto His marvellous light," is the design of the Church, then is the particular method here shown to have prevailed in the New Testament Church and practised in the Methodist Church, remarkably well adapted to this end. The select nature of the meeting as made up only of those who are avowedly de-

siring "to flee from the wrath to come, and to be
saved from their sins," secures unity of spirit and
aim. As followers of the risen Saviour they have mutual
joys and sorrows. What to the careless outside world
would be utterly unimportant, to them is intensely
interesting. The exercises of prayer and prophesying,
and fellowship and admonition are distasteful to the
unawakened, but to them they are pleasant and pro-
fitable. The ignorant are instructed, the weak are
strengthened, the sorowing are comforted. They bear
one another's burdens, they build one another up,
and so they fulfil the law of Christ. Here the new
convert can be watched over and guarded; here he can
be shielded from the evil influences which he has for-
saken, and from which he desires to be clear. He has
a home, he finds friends who are safe, he gets what his
soul longs for, and aided by its use he can grow up
into Christ, till he perfects holiness in the fear of
the Lord.

2. And while adapted to the end sought, it is also in
agreement with the instincts of human nature. Man
is a social being. Religion makes him more so. It
sanctifies this demand for society. The christian is
not left in perfect isolation in regard to the deep and
varied experiences of the love of God and his hope of
heaven, while he is permitted to have community of
feeling and intercourse on everything else. Religion
would, in such a case, war with the elements of our
nature that are not sinful, but necessary. Any plan of
Church organization which omits, or ignores this

characteristic of our nature, neglects to use one of the
most potent means of progress, and actually raises up
barriers to its acceptance. Church life ought to be
next, at any rate, to the domestic life, in its intimacy
and tenderness. Its highest attainments are possible
only by such means; and its most attractive manifes-
tations become possible by recognition of this most
loveable peculiarity of man's constitution.

3. It is a most striking confirmation of the correctness of the positions taken throughout this enquiry,
that in all ages the pious have been disposed to
practice what we have here shown to have been the
habits of the early disciples, acting under apostolic
countenance, guidance, and precept. David said,
" Come and hear, all ye that fear God, and I will
declare what He hath done for my soul ! " In the one
hundred and eleventh Psalm, there is admitted to be a
distinction between the " congregation " and the ' assembly of the upright."

The testimony of the prophet Malachi must be
received as indicating what was done in his day.
" Then, they that feared the Lord spake often one to
another, and the Lord hearkened and heard it; and a
book of remembrance was written before Him for
them that feared the Lord and thought upon His
name." After the early days of Christianity, when
this law of Christian life prevailed, whatever departure from this rule may have existed, it was a
departure from the practice of the golden age of the
Church. But still the best and most godly observed

the spirit of the rule long after the life of the Church
had declined. A modern writer,* on the subject, says,
" In fact, it was mainly by the communion of saints,
variously realized according to circumstances and
temperaments, in voluntary spiritual associations, that
living Christianity was preserved in the world by the
blessed Spirit of God ; and the historical continuity
of Christ's religion may be more satisfactorily sought
in these blessed fellowships, than in the concatenation
of bishops of every grade of holiness and heathenish-
ness, from the loftiest sanctity to the lowest depth of
worldliness and vice."

In the progress of early Christianity, it would
appear that the public and promiscuous, and then the
worldly assembly, became gradually substituted for
the loving, social, spiritual, and mutually edifying
assemblies that at first prevailed. Provision for the
propagation of Christianity, and even for public worship, may seem to conflict with the practice we here
show as pre-eminently Scriptural. The difficulty is
not real, and it is not within the purpose of this discussion to state its relation to the practice here ad-
vocated. Methodism has solved it by establishing the
Church meeting separate from the public congregation. But through the long ages the Church almost
totally ignored Christian fellowship—no doubt, because there was not enough spiritual life in her to
preserve it—and satisfied herself with the observance

---

*Rev. B. Gregory, in " The Holy Catholic Church."

of public worship, without the practical distinction
between believer and unbeliever. John Wesley's
recognition and adoption of actual christian fellowship, as a part of the true exercises of a Church, was
like the discovery of a lost art. Spiritually-minded
men, participating in its privileges, felt that apostolic
Christianity was restored. With it, the Church becomes more perfectly adapted to the wants and
peculiarities of human nature. It is, of course,
capable of abuse, but so also is every other good
thing.

Nor must the fallacy of voluntariness mislead us.
Admit that its beauty is in its voluntariness, still the
obligation abides. Holiness itself must be voluntary.
So is the celebration of the Lord's Supper; so is public
worship. But are these things, therefore, the less binding ? The law shows what is right, and it indicates
what is our privilege as well as our duty. All that is
necessary is to have hearts ready to enjoy our privileges, and our duties will be voluntary. In every
society there must be suitability of character for membership or else the duties of membership become irk-
some, and the society fails of its design. In the
matter of the Church, it is not enough that the persons
have suitability of character for membership ; they
must also maintain that membership, or else the
Church fails of its design. Let the living fires burn on
our altars, let the joyful christian experience of
primitive Christianity be in full possession among us,
and there will be little need to urge, either the Scrip-

tural character, or the usefulness of this divinely-
honoured means of grace.

SYNOPSIS.

We may now, before stating some particular benefits
of these rules, give a synopsis of the main points we
have endeavoured to maintain. As we have proceeded
in this enquiry, we have found that while the New
Testament speaks of the Church of God in its widest
sense as the "body of Christ," and including all who
are in the kingdom of God's grace; yet that it also and,
perhaps, more generally speaks of the Church in a
limited sense, as the community of believers,in any one
locality, meaning thereby such persons as were united
by the constraining influences of Christ's love, in distinct assemblies for the purpose of mutual edification.
That these assemblies were composed of believers who
could perform the ordinary duties of christian life,
and be subject to the law of the Church, to its discipline, to its obligation to propagate religion; and
could participate in its privileges. That the exercises
of these assemblies were those of prayer, prophesying,
reproving, comforting one another,fellowship, exercise
of discipline, and the breaking of bread. And that
these duties and privileges were mutual; all might
participate. All were to covet the gifts that in being
exercised would edify the Church. And we have seen
that these believers were encouraged and commanded
to attend these assemblies ; that they could not per-

form some of the most sacred duties nor enjoy some of the most precious privileges in their neglect. And we have also seen that the manner of entering into the membership of the Methodist Church and continuance therein are by the same principles and rules. That the christian life must be lived and the christian assembly of believers must be attended, and that this christian assembly or church-meeting—called a class-meeting—bears a close resemblance to the Primitive Church-meeting, so much so as to be practically identical. Its spirit and its exercises are similar. That-it is in harmony with the nature of inward religion as well as New Testament practice, and that it is also in harmony with the social instincts of our nature, and well calculated to build up in the most holy faith, all who use it.

And if these positions are supported by the testimony of the New Testament and the facts in the case, (a point we take it, that cannot be successfully gainsaid), then in the Methodist economy we have in the class-meeting a means of grace peculiarly christian, that needs to be maintained, and that should not be regarded as antagonistic to the tastes of any christian. And with these facts before us, it is not unscriptural to say to those of the Methodist fold, you must meet your brethren here, that you may bear your part and receive your needed help and edification ; that we may know whether you can rightly sit down with us to the Supper of the Lord ; and that you may be present for that express purpose—

"He bids us build each other up ;
And gathered into one,
To our high calling's glorious hope
We hand in hand go on.

" The gift which he on one bestows,
We all delight to prove ;
The grace through every vessel flows,
In purest streams of love."

CHAPTER VI.

THE ADVANTAGES OF SUCH a METHOD.

*What are the Advantages and Benefits of this Rule?
May Appropriately Close this Discussion.*

WE may now profitably look at some of the advantages that this Scriptural method has in connection with the ends which the Church has in view ; and we may mark the benefits which flow from its observance. God always employs appropriate and effectual means to accomplish His purposes ; and these means are always in harmony with the ends to be reached. We may be sure His unerring Spirit led the disciples to adopt the practices which we have found to be indicated in the New Testament. By this means there is agreement between the teachings of inspired apostles and the work of the Holy Spirit in His people. It thus becomes confirming evidence of the law of religious fellowship which we maintain. It is in harmony with the spirit and ultimate re-

sults of Christianity. Standing before us as a whole we
see how it breaks down the barriers that separate
men. Under its benign influence they are drawn into
closer communion with each other ; they become much
more deeply interested in each other's well-being; and
then they become desirous of aiding the object of
their affection.   Here is seen at once one of the most
important advantages and benefits of the practice of
christian fellowship, viz. :—

1. It presents a practical manifestation of the
love of the brethren, enjoined by Christ.   " Love one
another" is His command.   " By this shall all men
know that ye are my disciples, because ye have
love one to another." We do not repel those whom we
love.   We do not seek to cover up every emotion of
the heart, nor to hold them ignorant of every subject
that interests us.   We do not look on them with a
cold and careless glance.   It constrains us to be near
them ; to seek their society, and to rejoice in it.   This
was what cemented the first christians.   It was proof
of the presence of a power never before operating on
them.   The love of the brotherhood that would not
have done this might, from what we know of human
nature, have led us to doubt whether a new and divine
life had been begotten in them.   It was a Scriptural
evidence of conversion : " We know that we have
passed from death unto life because we love the
brethren."   Community of feeling and interest makes
them show their love one to another.   This simple,
social, and yet spiritual and rational way of ex-

pressing this love of the brotherhood organized the Church.

Nothing could be more reasonable than that men under such powerful influences, and having such high aims should by mutual counsel and fellowship seek to cherish these influences and promote these aims. Shut out from the world, their union is close and sacred. The world sees a cementing 'process that proves the presence of a divine power. God is honoured thereby. To have gone on in their ordinary courses even with renewed lives, would not have accomplished so much to arrest the attention of men and exalt Christ.

The same unity of spirit and aim exists in christians to-day, and should bind them together.. The world is alien. So the same proof of interest in, and love to Christ and His followers are expressed by this close union of christian fellowship in this form of Church meeting. It is, indeed, the union of saints.

2. The securing of a more intimate association on the part of believers and as a consequence greater compactness of organization is a benefit of great importance. The Church needs to be organically knit together. With its spirit and character right, it has power to influence the world. It becomes more conspicuous and is better fitted to shed light upon the world. If the organic life is thus produced it will become distinct from all beside and will be admired and loved. The invisible Church is not an organization and cannot be directly employed to do any definite work. But the organic Church can be thus employed,

provided she is pervaded with such life as makes her conscious of her privilege and duty. For this possession of common life it must be united to its head—Christ—in all its members, so that they shall have mutual sympathy. Then the "effectual working in the measure in every part" becomes a possibility. The body is seen and the character of its life is known. That secret and cementing power of love which binds them all together finds its true expression. They love each other and are all interested in each other's condition. Love finds its proper exercise. And as their numbers multiply the continuance of this brotherly concern becomes possible only by classification. If they never met separate from the promiscuous company they could not be organically distinguished from them. There would rise the danger of true believers not being always readily distinguished from the world. The church made up in this way, and professedly standing forth in this form, can be just what she wills to be. She need bear no responsibility that does not properly belong to her. She is then the company of the faithful, and may be known in her true character, without the stain of unnecessary worldliness.

They are a distinct body of such as place themselves where they can best live the life they profess to desire to live. Those who will not identify themselves fully with their aims and interests, drop from this organization. Provision is thus made, as by a law of its life, for the Church to drop off its dead branches.

3. Benefit comes again from the means of developing

E

and utilizing the varied gifts of the Church, which this form of Church life provides. The common brotherhood makes the obligation of mutual edification comparatively easy. The varied exercises under so little of restraint, save what the spirit and aim of their assembly imposes, gives occasion for every variety of natural endowment to be utilized. Whether the gift of song or of speech is possessed it may be used to the profit of all, and in being used may grow. Many a mighty warrior in the army of the living God has acquired great boldness in the faith What otherwise might have remained dormant, or even unknown has been stirred into activity by the excitment of this holy fellowship. Let the idea of Church life be merely the public congregation of promiscuous elements, presided over, and its worship conducted by one gifted man, and there is but little room for the employment of the varied talents of the Church. Only by making occasion can they be either known or employed. But by this plan even, the normal condition of things is continually bringing to the surface every form of gift enjoyed by any member of the society. Such has been the fact in connection with the existence of this form of Church life in Methodism. The gifts of prayer, of exhortation, of song, of sympathy, and of sound judgment are all available, and have the best opportunity to be employed for the building up of the Church of God. Herein is found one of the secrets of the progress of Christianity in connection with those who have followed this Scriptural method.

4. But it is not alone, or even mainly, in the line of natural gifts that this plan is found so beneficial. In the line of the graces of the varied members of the Church, there is even greater advantage from this rule of action. The strong can help the weak; the wise can instruct the ignorant; the courageous can inspire the timid; the joyful can cheer the sorrowful. Many are the varied graces of the Divine Spirit bestowed on the Church of God; but ever that they may be used for the edification of all. Like the varied members of the human body, every one of them is necessary, and may serve the others. "And the eye cannot say unto the hand, I have no need of thee; nor, again, the head to the feet, I have no need of you." Every grace may be used in this spiritual brotherhood, and finds a ready means of operation in such form of regular association. In such a body "the members should have the same care one for another." The feeblest young converts of the flock can be nurtured, and even carried, if need be, till they "all come in the unity of the faith, and of the knowledge of the Son of God, unto a perfect man, unto the measure of the stature of the fulness of Christ." So it has often been, and so, in the ordering of God this Christian fellowship was designed to be the means of building up the Church of God.

Fuller knowledge of the deep things of God becomes possible to each, by his more intimate knowledge of what another has received. New inspiration to press forward is gained from the exhortation, or from the joy, or from the heavenly mindedness with which he comes in contact. Isolation could not possibly accomplish such ends ; so the over-ruling Spirit has guided to a better order of things; and the communion of saints has become a living reality.

Both the graces of the Spirit bestowed on the brotherhood, and the loving association of these disciples, are a mighty instrumentality to help the soul in its spiritual struggles. These come betimes to all. The inexperienced need counsel. The timid need protection. Those downcast need lifting up. What better method could exist than the Church meeting we have shown to be the the New Testament ideal of the local Church, for such a purpose. The nature of the thing assures us of its adaptation to such purposes ; and the experience in our own time in all the branches of Methodism has demonstrated its importance.

Can all this be true, and there be no ground for believing in a divine ordering ? And does not such a fact greatly strengthen the testimony we have produced for this method of Church life and operation ? The Scripture evidence needs no such support as matter of proof; but the fact serves to give completeness to the picture presented for our observation. And it may serve to reconcile some opposing thought, that still holds its sway from the force of education in another direction on this subject. Devout gratitude becomes us for such perfect provision for the spiritual needs of all classes of souls gathered into the spiritual fold.

5. And is it not also a most effective means for
preserving the purity and spirituality of the Church?
The accomplishing of such an end is not only im-
mensely important, but exceedingly difficult. Provision can be made for expulsion of open trans-
gressors without any very great difficulty, though,
even its execution is no easy matter. But how can
the Church, in its organic form, take cognizance of the
spiritual condition of its membership? is a most
difficult problem. I believe that this is the most
perfect method that it is possible to adopt. It starts
on the spiritual basis, pure and simple. It promotes
it to the largest degree. It repels in its whole operation all worldly-mindedness; so that it becomes a very
unnatural thing for the man of the world to seek such
association. He has no sympathy with it. He is an
utter alien to its spirit, its life, and practices. He can
have no satisfaction or enjoyment in such a place.
As soon as the soul that was alive and interested
in its work becomes dead, the thing becomes dull,
and then distasteful. Then, following his own in-
clinations, he absents himself, and thereby declares
himself no longer of this brotherhood. Expulsion.
if you choose to call it such, is his own act, and is a
most tangible expression of his lack of suitable
qualifications for such a position. The nature of the
conditions of this membership becomes, thereby, a
most effective means of preserving the spirituality
and purity of the visible Church. Any failure that
becomes conspicuous arises mainly from failure to

apply the rule. Nominal membership is thus produced, and is the measure of departure from the New
Testament rule of membership. This is the exact
fact in regard to Methodism; and it is full of
argument in support of the position maintained in
these pages. It is also very admonitory. Just in
proportion as the membership has been a practical,
fellowship membership, have there been spiritual life
and power. The production and maintenance of
these are the great ends to be served by the Church's
operations.

6. The last advantage I shall mention, as especially
growing out of this manner of maintaining Church
membership, is the excellency of the means by which
it provides for taking hold of those, who, by the
power of the truth and the Spirit of God, are awakened to a sense of sin, and desire to be saved. The
evangelistic work of the Church can, and does go on
in its public preaching; and, by this means, public
worship is maintained. And, although the worldly do
not worship, they do come to the place of the holy,
where God's people worship him. Here they are
reached by the truth, and are awakened; and, if also
saved, can find a congenial home in the assembly of
the " saints." But if they are seeking the Lord, there
is no better place for them to be led forward, till
" Christ has wrought a perfect cure," than the class-
meeting. Here they are surrounded with men and
women, who know the way, and who are prepared to
instruct and guide them. Spiritual interests are here

stronger than in any other place they can find. Often
they rise to what is sometimes called a white heat.
Every member there is interested in their case. Prayer,
fervent and appropriate, is made for their salvation.
Experience of those who have, like themselves, tasted
the wormwood and the gall, is heard. Sympathy for
them in their intense longings for peace and pardon is
felt, as only pardoned souls can feel it. With such
advantages surrounding them, and in full use, if they
are safe anywhere on earth they are safe there.

CONCLUSION.

And does the Church exist to enlighten, and then to
gather in the world? Must she not only rouse the
slumbering, but save them? Then, here is a means
well adapted to help her in so high a work. Here
she may work to best advantage on well understood
and pre-eminently suitable lines. All her glorious
aims may be promoted in her own divinely-sanctioned
means. Here she gathers all her trophies, that they
may speak with tongues of fire the wonderful works
of God. Here, all the natural instincts, sanctified by
grace, are made to serve the highest ends of man's
existence. The divine promise is, indeed, fulfilled in
the experience of those, thus gathered in Christ's
name; and while saints are built up in their most holy
faith, God is abundantly glorified.

With such facts before us, it is surely impossible to
doubt the Divine appointment of such methods in the

Church of God, for the perfecting of the saints. Their perfect agreement with the genius of Christianity; and the general, uniform participation in them by the early christians strongly suggest that any thing like distaste of them now, must arise from want of the true spirit of religion. And all who are striving to war the good warfare and lay hold on eternal life, may be devoutly thankful that such aids are afforded them in the glorious strife.

FINIS.

PRINTED AT THE "GUARDIAN" OFFICE, TORONTO.